Introduction

How to Improve Your Memory is divided into two sections. The first section is called, "Mnemonics, Memory Palaces and More" and the second is, "Flash Cards". The first section will provide an excellent introduction to a variety of memory techniques – the second section, "flash cards", will give you an effective overall framework for learning a course or large body of information. Integrate the mnemonic and other ideas from section one into your flash cards to create a still more effective learning system.

So, without further ado, let's begin your crash course and build up your greatest asset: your mind!

Section 1 of How to Improve Your Memory and Remember Anything – Mnemonics, Memory Palaces and More

Mnemonics and How We Have Evolved to Remember Things

The human mind has not been able to evolve as quickly as the developments of the world around it. How we live now differs dramatically from how we lived just a hundred years ago. By looking back a thousand years, or further, we can see even more drastic changes to lifestyle and environment.

The simple fact is that the things we ask of our minds today are very different from what we asked of them in previous generations. There are qualitative and quantitative differences to how we need to use our minds in the 21st century. However, our minds have not had time to evolve and adapt to these new expectations, and therefore often struggle to perform.

The types of information that we used to want to memorize predominantly contained directions, images, and feelings. These were the things most important to survival and what we most often asked our minds to memorize.

In the modern world, however, there are many things we need to remember that do not fall into these categories, like formulas and phone numbers. These are not easy for the human mind to memorize because it is only relatively recently in human history that these demands have been placed on our minds.

Phone numbers, for example, are an essential part of everyday life, but most of us are hopeless at remembering a number sequence that long in a short space of time. Most people require multiple failed attempts and corrections to commit a number sequence to memory. This is because a ten digit code is quite alien to a human mind still expecting to hunt and forage for food.

To memorize a phone number initially, the best most of us can manage is to simply focus on the number and try to force it into our memory. However, this is not working alongside the strengths of the human mind and so is not an effective approach.

Memorizing a list of groceries, another daily memorization task in our world, is also a struggle. Although remembering a few objects is doable, memorizing seven or more items is difficult for most. This is because memorization of lists is another task our ancestors rarely had to perform, so such a feat does not play to the strengths of the human mind.

Understanding that our minds have developed strengths and weaknesses and learning where these originated is a solid foundation to using memorization tools. Indeed, all of the techniques in this book can be better understood from this premise: for better memorization, we need to utilize the strengths of the human mind. By manipulating information that is difficult to memorize, you can re-frame numbers, lists, dates, and formulas to make them easier to commit to memory.

Mnemonics: Playing to the Mind's Strengths and How to Remember Anything

A mnemonic device changes a chunk of information from something difficult to remember (something we are poorly developed to retain, e.g., a phone number), into something easier to remember (and that we are better developed to remember).

We will go through various mnemonic techniques in the following chapters. All of them work to engage your mind in a way that plays to its strengths. You have probably had some previous experience with mnemonic devices. You may already be using some in your day-to-day life. A few, though not nearly enough, are taught in schools.

In this book, you will also learn how to create your own mnemonic devices so you can make learning boring, difficult information fun and easy. It will be the difference between night and day. Memorizing material will begin to feel like swimming through water instead of treacle.

Mnemonic Tip 1: Create a Rhyme

It is easier to remember a phrase of words rather than a list of things. Even easier is remembering a phrase that rhymes, because a rhyme creates a stronger memory than a list of objects.

An excellent example is how people in England recall how many days are in each month. The rhyme goes:

"Thirty days hath September, April June and November.

All the rest have thirty-one.

Excepting February alone,

And that has twenty-eight days clear,

And twenty nine in each leap year."

Remembering how many days are in each month is significantly easier using this rhyme than solely a list of months and numbers.

Even just the first two lines of the rhyme allow for an easy recollection of the number of days in most of the months in the year.

Another famous rhyming mnemonic is "righty tighty, left loosey." This tells us which way we need to turn a screw driver in order to tighten or loosen a screw. The phrase is so simple that it is tough to forget.

These are just two examples of how rhyming can be used to manipulate information, making it more memorable. Work to create your own rhymes. The simpler they are, the better.

Mnemonic Tip 2: Convert Digits into Words

Remembering phrases is easier than remembering a series of digits. Similarly, whole words are easier to remember than single letters. By converting single digits or letters into whole words and then constructing them into sentences that are memorable, you can much more effectively memorize a list of numbers. This is because there is no meaning or reference point to a single number or letter, so they don't make a significant impression on our minds.

Actors can remember whole scripts and some manage to retain these for the rest of their lives. They can do this because the words and the phrases have such a clear meaning to them. The script comprises rich stories and interesting characters; a life the actor is going to inhabit. If they tried to remember the same amount of information in the form of only numbers or letters, they would have no chance.

This is an important aspect to every mnemonic device: the modification of material from that of lesser meaning to something of greater meaning.

For example, we can turn the number sequence 0 1 8 2 4 into the phrase "Only One Crate of beer tonight for me." Here, I have converted the numbers into words in the following way:

Only= 0 or Zero (the sound, "oh," here prompts us to the number)

One= One (we are using the same word / number)

Crate=eight (I am using a phonetically similar word here, but still, this is more than enough to make it memorable, and allows a clear link to the number 8)

Tonight= Two (as above, except now the first syllable of the word is the same as the number we want to remember)

For= Four (here we are using two words that sound the same)

This was a straightforward mnemonic device for the memorization of just five digits. For a longer series of digits, such as a whole phone number, the same process can be applied. Take time to practice this on your own phone number now. Or perhaps pick a random series of digits, and then re-code it into a sentence.

It will seem difficult at first, but with a practice you can quickly become adept at this method.

This exact process can also be applied to letters. Perhaps the letters H P become the words "Harry Potter," so, if you wanted to remember the code 01824HP, you could encode it into the phrase:

'"Only one crate of beer tonight for me." said Harry Potter.'

Read the sentence a few times aloud and visualize the scene in your mind. Imagine Harry Potter sitting at a bar drinking beer. He says, "Only one crate of beer tonight, for me," and burps loudly. Imagining the visual of this will root the phrase deeply to your memory. Odd visuals such as this also play to your mind's strengths. This, combined with a predominance to phrases, will mean that you can more effectively remember 0 1 8 2 4 H P than merely trying to focus on it. Indeed, you might find that this visual, the phrase, and by extension the number/letter sequence sticks in your mind for years to come.

Mnemonic Tip 3: How to Remember a Lists of Words

To better memorize a list of words, the goal again is to modify something that has little meaning into something which has a lot of meaning. An example of a series of words to remember might be if you were trying to remember the Great Lakes, in order, looking from left to right on a map.

The Great Lakes are:

Superior, Michigan, Huron, Erie, and Ontario.

It is not straightforward / natural to remember these five words in order because there is no meaning and no relationship between how they are ordered. Therefore, we need to encode them into something which does have meaning: a phrase. A popular phrase for this is:

"Superman helps everyone."

This is a very straightforward phrase but holds the information for where the Great Lakes are geographically. The phrase encodes the first letter of each of the Great Lakes into each syllable of the sentence. To clarify:

Super = S = Superior

Man = M = Michigan

Helps = H = Huron

Every = E = Erie

One = O = Ontario

The phrase also works well as a prompt for remembering the names of the lakes themselves. Remembering the phrase, and therefore the first letter of each lake's name, will often be enough to draw out the whole word from your memory. This is another key idea in memorization: information is linked, or bound together, in our mind.

And so, within a minute we can go from knowing none of the Great Lakes to knowing all of them and being able to point them out on a map. This is all due to the power of encoding/modifying information from something which has little meaning into something which has a lot of meaning.

Mnemonic Tip 4: Create a Story

The phrase we created earlier, "'Only one crate of beer tonight for me,' said Harry Potter," encoded the number/letter sequence 01824HP into something easy to memorize because the phrase contains easy to grasp, memorable, and linked concepts. This all comes as a result of what was before meaningless information, feeding into another aspect of memorization: the power of storytelling.

The previous phrase could be the beginning of a story if you wanted to memorize a longer number/letter sequence. Creating a story will powerfully root the information and its order into your memory. It only takes adding a series of phrases to the above sentence to build what could be a long sequence that would otherwise be very difficult to remember.

Here is another set of random numbers with two letters on the end:

36829AK

Try and create your own phrase using the above series and add it onto the code/story we have already created with Harry Potter. Make this new phrase run on and tell a story. Be patient if words and a phrase don't leap out at once. Remember to link the numbers to letters by using rhymes. Try to have fun with it and embrace your inner storyteller! Being able to quickly encode information in this way will serve you well for life, so stick with it.

Mnemonic Tip 5: Rooting to Visual Memories to Create a Memory Palace

The human mind is excellent at imagining locations familiar to us. This was important for the survival of our ancestors, and indeed still is for us today, to be able to clearly recall the layout of an area and our homes. We have adapted to be able to remember and visualize locations very well.

Creating a memory palace uses this powerful asset to encode information that is hard to remember into something that utilizes geographical and visual memories and plays to our mind's strengths. This creates something easy to remember that was previously very difficult.

First, choose a location you know well. This might be your home, where you grew up, your old school, or maybe your place of work. Now, let's try to encode a simple grocery list into a story within your chosen location.

The list is:

Cheese

Chicken

Eggs

Potatoes

Tomatoes

Pineapple

Now I will walk you through an example story that roots the above list to locations in my home, thus creating a memory palace.

I walk through the front door and see a mouse eating cheese in the hallway. Then a chicken eats the mouse and rushes up the stairs. I chase after it, but as I do, potatoes begin rolling down the stairs and I have to dodge past them. At the top of the stairs, I go into my bedroom where there is a tomato lying in my bed. It tells me that it wants to go on holiday to a beach where we can eat pineapples together.

Yes, this short story is absolutely ridiculous, and you might now be worried for my mental health. But this sequence of events powerfully roots the shopping list to locations in my mind, and because the memory palace is my own home (which I know very well), I can easily imagine these absurd things occurring. I have now rooted a series of random objects into a story as well as onto visual memories I already have. I will now remember this list (for better or worse) for a good deal of time to come.

If you have a series of separate lists to remember, use a series of palaces. This will root the order of the list more powerfully to a certain location and allow you to recall the lists separately. This is how people can memorize the order of a dozen separate decks of playing cards. They create a dozen different Memory Palaces which they can enter separately.

The memory palace is excellent for remembering a list and its order because we are creating a sequential journey within the palace. I used the example of a shopping list, in which the order is unimportant. Whether you use it for ordered or unordered lists, creating a memory palace is an excellent way to remember a large amount of information that is otherwise difficult to remember.

General Tips on Using Mnemonics and Optimizing the Recall of Encoded Information

There are a few important rules of thumb that will make the information you encode more memorable.

1. Make things absurd and funny.

Things that are everyday or boring simply don't stick in the mind as much as something that is humorous and ridiculous. The list 'cat, eggs, and horse' could be re-imagined into a cat eating eggs whilst riding a horse. By being so outrageous, this image sticks in the mind more powerfully than something mundane. It also makes the encoding process easier and more fun! Try to think like a child and get creative in making your images, phrases, and stories as downright ridiculous and funny as you can.

2.   Don't use more ideas than necessary.

A series of mundane events is much harder to remember than one ridiculous event. Therefore, try to compound and collapse words and ideas into the essential few. Less is easier to remember.

3.   Utilize all the senses.

The mind remembers things more effectively when every sense is involved. The sense of smell in particular is a powerful sense that is rooted deeply to emotion and memory. If you create a mental scene in which you can smell eggs as well as see them, you will create a stronger impact on your mind, and make "eggs" easier to remember. Similarly, use the other senses to create a memory that is more vivid than just a visual.

4.   Strengthen relationships to group information.

When remembering a list of items or when you want to relate sets of things together, there are a few things you can do to strengthen their relationships, thereby also strengthening the memory. An example might be to collapse words/objects onto each other. Alternatively, depict words/objects eating one another to cement their connection. You can also wrap objects around one another or imagine objects chasing or melting into each other. Use your imagination. Anything that might occur between two objects can be used to join two things and better encode information.

Remembering People's Names

One of the most common memory improvements people desire is to become better at remembering names. It is a very common problem that we have all experienced – that moment when you know you have been told someone's name, but you simply cannot recall it.

As a social principle, we intuitively know remembering someone's name is important. There is something intrinsically valuable in a name. We like to hear our own name and feel a little slighted when someone doesn't remember it. It is embarrassing, frustrating even, when we are on the other end and can't remember a name we know we have been told.

Learning a few tricks will help you dramatically improve how well you remember names. These techniques will ensure you make better impressions, as you will never forget someone's name again. Everyone likes hearing their name, and as you begin to remember everyone you have met, even distant acquaintances you met long ago, you will notice how pleased people are as you easily repeat their name back to them.

There is a lot in a name, and with a few simple tricks, remembering the name of everyone you meet is something you can now master.

Why is it so Difficult to Remember a Name?

You are not alone if you struggle to remember names. Many people find it difficult to repeat a name they have heard just moments after they heard it. But why is this? After all, a name is a very short piece of information. Shouldn't it be easy to remember? The name is also usually a word we have heard before. For example, if you live in the USA and meet someone called "Tom", this is a popular name and only a three-letter word. How can "Tom" be difficult to remember?

The main reason for this memory goof is that when you meet someone for the first time, there is actually a great deal of tension and subconscious activity within your mind. Psychologically and physiologically we are programmed to quickly assess this person and decide whether they are a potential friend or foe, or even a potential mate, as well as simply whether this is someone we can like and trust. All of these things cloud our mental activity, so it becomes tough to engage our conscious mind, which is essential if we are to remember even a small piece of information, such as a name.

Another reason is that, when meeting someone for the first time, part of the conscious mind is engaged in deciding what it is you are going to say to this new person. Simple decisions take up conscious energy. You must make the decision of what greeting to use, whether you will shake their hand or not, or perhaps whether you will compliment them on the shoes they are wearing. All of these thoughts and questions need to be resolved, leaving little left for the memorization of a name.

The initial moments of meeting someone become so full of mental and physiological activity that memorization of even a short, simple name is very difficult. You have a finite amount of mental capacity, and if you leave it to its own devices, your mind will not focus sufficiently on the name you heard.

However, despite these obstacles, it is possible to become fantastically good at remembering names. Let's look at a few tricks that will make this process easier.

Remembering Names Trick 1: Pay Attention

As I just explained, our attention is normally diffused when we first meet someone. It is decidedly *not* focused on listening to and memorizing their name. A powerful way to improve memorization of names is to simply force our attention onto the name and focus consciously on it at the expense of other thoughts.

Indeed, conscious focus is always a powerful tool to increase our ability to remember things. However, when remembering names in particular, it can make all the difference because it is only a small word that requires recollection, and only the obstacle of diffused attention needs to be overcome.

Now, your focus does not have to be at the exclusion of everything else. All that is needed is a few seconds focusing primarily on the name. Do not worry about seeming distracted for a moment during the initial greeting period. A much better impression will be made if you remember the person's name five minutes later.

Remembering Names Trick 2: Internal and External Repetition

As with memorizing anything, the simple method of repetition will be of help when remembering names. The more you consciously expose your mind to a person's name, the more deeply the memory will entrench in your mind.

The easiest way to do this is to simply repeat the name in your mind a few times. So, if you meet someone called "Tom," simply repeat, "Tom, Tom, Tom, Tom, Tom" in your mind. This will create a stronger memory than hearing it just once.

A more powerful iteration of this principle is to repeat it externally in conversation. In this case you could simple say, "Tom. It's nice to meet you, Tom." Saying this short phrase repeats the word twice aloud. Saying things aloud creates a more powerful memory than only thinking it. The choice to say the word, mouthing it, and hearing yourself say it comprises a series of small events that increase memorization more than if you simply repeated the words in your mind. Continuing to repeat the name throughout conversation will further cement it in your memory. Don't repeat the person's name so many times that you sound crazy. Just say it whenever you have the opportunity to do so naturally.

The final way to apply this principle is to ask the person to repeat their name. To do this, simply pretend you didn't hear their name and ask them to say it again. Here, again, you are building a stronger memory by re-affirming the name.

You may have more trouble memorizing a name if it originated in a culture or country that is foreign to you. If this is the case, don't be too proud to ask them how to pronounce their name to clarify the sounds of the name (and, of course, to hear it twice). Then, repeat the name back to them to confirm your pronunciation is correct. The repetition and affirmation of the sounds in this short exchange will help you to memorize their name. Moreover, the correct pronunciation of someone's name can be just as important as remembering it at all. Therefore, taking the time to ensure you pronounce it correctly will separate you from other people this person has met who perhaps misinterpreted their name, making a still better impression.

Remembering Names Trick 3: Create Links

Another powerful way to guarantee you remember someone's name is to link/connect/anchor the name to a person you know with the same name. This works in a similar manner to previous mnemonic techniques, such as the memory palace, and associates the new information to information that you have already memorized.

You can create an even more vivid connection by using other memory principles. Perhaps create a moving, dynamic scene in your mind that is colorful and humorous to join this person to the person you already know. If you want to remember the person you have just met, "Tom," perhaps visualize the Tom you already know playing soccer with the new Tom you have just met. To make it more memorable, perhaps imagine them playing soccer with an egg. Do whatever it takes. It doesn't have to be especially clever, just memorable and unique.

It might sound excessive to create this scene and build an association to a memory of someone you already know. But creating and imagining this scene will only take a few moments, and once you have established it, you can guarantee the name of the person you have just met will be locked into your memory.

Never Lose Your Keys Again

Another common memory issue people have is misplacing items. For many of us, there are certain items that just keep getting lost. The quintessential lost item is the set of keys. If you haven't personally experienced this, I can almost guarantee you have a friend or family member who has, at some point, rushed through the house turning over anything and everything, only to eventually turn to you and ask exasperatedly, "Have you seen my keys? I can't find them anywhere!" Losing things is a common problem, and is another example of where better understanding of our memory and application of simple techniques can help us immensely.

Losing important items, like keys, is very frustrating, perhaps because it seems bizarre that we can lose something so central to our lives. We know we will need them again, so why can't we remember where they are? The answer is this: our habits simply don't support how important the item is. We never take the time to remember where we put them.

Losing our keys is better understood as a manner of disorganization rather than not being aware of their importance. It is not due to a bad memory, either. It is simply because when we go into "autopilot" mode and stop being consciously aware of what we are doing, we put the keys in an odd place.

So, how can we stop doing this and learn to always know where our keys (and all the other things we need) are?

Becoming more organized with where we put these objects is the easiest answer. If you often lose your keys, create a habit of always putting them in a bowl by your front door. Every time you enter your house, put the keys into this bowl, and then they will always be there when you need them. This will take some effort at first. For at least a week (a habit often takes at least seven repetitions before it becomes ingrained) you will need to do this every time you come in through the front door. Soon the habit will become second nature and the keys will always be in the bowl when you need them.

If you regularly misplace your keys, this could be just the tip of a greater disorganization that runs through your life. Similarly, the deeper cause could be utilizing very little conscious focus throughout your day-to-day life. Perhaps you are spending most of your energy trying to retain focus in other areas, leaving little to no focus for staying aware of where you put your keys. If this sounds at all possible, save yourself the stress and consider working on focus and organization elsewhere in your life.

Did I Leave the Oven On?

Another common memory problem, similar to losing keys, is forgetting whether we have done something (an important, necessary action) and then fretting endlessly over it. This may take the form of forgetting whether we turned the oven off, locked the front door, or unplugged the iron. Often, indeed usually, we have completed these things, but nonetheless we get stressed and cannot recall with certainty what we did.

Occasionally forgetting whether we have done one of these things is unavoidable. We cannot always be perfectly aware of what we have just done; at times there are just too many pressures on us to be mindful of everything. However, if you regularly forget whether you have done something or often feel a pang of uncertainty, the following techniques can remedy this issue. These techniques can also be applied to the previous problem of not remembering where you put your keys.

In whatever activity you want to be more mindful of, if you make a stronger memory of performing the action, you will remember what you have done with increased clarity. You will then ensure a greater confidence when recalling what you have done (or where you put your keys).

To do this, simply repeat to yourself the action you are doing out loud a few times. And so, if you regularly feel uncertainty over whether you locked the front door, for one week make the effort to affirm out loud (or in your head if you fear odd looks from neighbors) every time you lock it by saying, "I am locking the front door." For losing your keys, this takes the form of stating: "I am putting my keys in my pocket," or perhaps, "I am putting my keys on the table," each time you perform these actions.

Repetition creates a stronger memory, as does verbally stating it, so do both to make sure you never forget what you have done. The principle is always the same: create a stronger memory of what you have done and in turn you will never forget. But don't worry; you won't have to do this for the rest of your life. Just by doing this a few times you will become mindful of the tasks you complete and start remembering whether you turned the oven off or not.

"Fishing" For Memories

Another common memory problem is the inability to recall something that has been memorized. It has probably happened to you at some point: the feeling that you certainly know the answer to a question, but no matter how hard you try, you simply cannot remember it. Or perhaps the nagging feeling that there is something you were meant to remember, something important, but it simply won't come to mind. There are a few simple techniques that can help you to retrieve these "lost memories." I will apply the analogy of fishing to explain these techniques because the two share many similarities.

In order to "fish" out a memory, you need to first decide on the bait you will use to lure the memory from the recesses of your mind. As I have stated before, the mind works powerfully by association. So, by consciously letting your mind linger on memories that are closely related to what you are trying to remember (the closer, the better) you can wait for the memory to "bite" onto the bait through association.

There are many different kinds of "bait" you can use to evoke a lost memory. If it is something that you were thinking about earlier in the day, retrace the steps your mind went through. Focus on the things you were thinking about around the time of the memory. Let your mind go through the same motions it did earlier and, with a bit of luck, your mind will re-find the memory previously lost.

If you are trying to remember a certain word, another form of "bait" you can use is running through the letters of the alphabet consecutively from A-Z. When you land on the letter that begins the word, your mind will be encouraged to rediscover the forgotten word. For each letter, pause for a moment and let your mind relax. Visualize words beginning with the letter and lightly hold the intention of recalling the word.

A physical way of "baiting" your mind is to physically return to a location or expose yourself to a sensory experience that is related to the lost memory. For example, if you were at your desk at work when you discovered the name of a local business you need to contact (but whose name you now cannot remember), returning to your desk may prompt you to recall the name of the business. Again, this is thanks to the associative power of our memories.

Tricks like running through the alphabet in the attempt to find the first letter of the word can be applied to many pieces of information you want to rediscover. The best "bait" will be as close as possible in relation to the lost memory.

You can use multiple forms of bait to increase the likelihood of recalling the lost memory. For example, return to your desk and then also use the alphabet method.

Working to recall memories by "fishing" with "bait" is similar to real fishing in that you also need to be patient. It may take just moments, or it may take much longer. The more you relax and expect to recall the memory in time, without letting yourself become frustrated and impatient, the more likely it is you will be able to "fish" the memory out. Just like real fishing, you need to choose the right bait and have patience.

Relax and Focus

Whenever you use your memory, whether it is studying or attempting to recall a piece of information, it is important to keep your mind relaxed. If you can combine this with a focused mind, you will be able to improve how effectively your mind operates. These two aspects will improve both memorization and recall. If you are trying to memorize or recall material whilst feeling a lot of tension and/or stress, your mind will not work nearly as effectively. It is therefore important to work in a relaxed and focused mode. The following are a few techniques and principles that can help you achieve this.

An important part of staying relaxed is not putting unneeded pressure on your mind. Whether you are memorizing or recalling material, do not strain your mind or become frustrated or desperate to make it happen. This might not always be possible, but still, make it the norm to not put your mind under strain. Instead, work to make the process consistently easy and light.

This is especially important if you find yourself coming up against a "wall" and cannot remember what you want to. Here, the more you push, the less likely you will be to remember. If you come up against a "wall" and simply cannot recall what you want, consider taking a break and expect it to return to your mind at a later date. This expectation, and almost forgetting about the problem, will help turn the impasse over to your subconscious for it to work on instead.

In order to improve your attention and focus, it is helpful to control and create an environment that helps you to think more effectively. Depending on how well you currently concentrate and what your habits are, it might help to experiment working in different locations. Consider social places, as well as working alone. Some people find that working at a library with others around them helps to pressure them into studying and working hard as well. Others find themselves distracted too easily with others around them. Experiment and find what works best for you.

Also, make sure that you have quiet if you need it and that if you are listening to music, it never distracts you. It might help to use earplugs to completely block out sound. Earplugs often come in handy at the end of the workweek, when what was previously an acceptably noisy office becomes a distraction and a drain on the last ebbs of mental energy that you have. Here, earplugs can be the small but meaningful boost to your ability to concentrate.

Having an ordered and tidy workspace can also help you to concentrate, making you feel as clear and focused as the space around you.

Another way to improve your concentration is to become more relaxed and physically present. The most important part of this is sitting comfortably with good posture. Slouching or sitting uncomfortably will compromise how well you can concentrate and may of course lead to health problems later in life. If you are working at a computer, ensure the screen is at a proper height so as to avoid unnecessarily straining your neck.

If you are preparing to work on material or recalling material, take a few moments to clear and calm your mind. Imagining a dark sky or perhaps an empty room will help empty your head of thoughts. Try counting slowly backwards from ten whilst concentrating on your breathing.

Practicing all these small tricks will come together to make a real improvement on how well you concentrate, relax and focus. In turn, you will dramatically increase your memorization and recall abilities.

Re-Form Material to Remember It

A powerful way to improve the memorization of material (which is particularly useful if you are studying a course with a rote curriculum) is the regular practice of re-forming material into your own words. This simply means presenting the same material in a different way. This might be re-writing it so that it is phrased differently, or perhaps turning it into a series of pictures. Re-forming material will help to improve your understanding and memorization of material.

When we re-form material, we are forcing our minds to engage with the material in a deeper way. It is impossible to recall and recreate material if we don't understand it well. The more clearly we understand something, the better we will remember it. This is because with deeper understanding comes more detailed and meaningful connections between the material within the brain.

There are many ways to become proficient at reworking material to make it your own. By simply taking notes in class, you are changing the information from one form to another. Note taking is the process of picking out a topic's most important parts and then recording it on paper. This is an act of re-forming material. And so, by taking notes in class, you will improve your understanding and memorization of the material.

Choosing a medium that is significantly different from the original medium is perhaps the best way to boost understanding and memorization of the material. For example, if you are reading a journal that you want to memorize, consider re-forming the most important elements of it into a mind map or maybe put them into flash card form. This will create many new connections within your mind because you are forcing the information to separate and reform in a significant manner.

The most obvious time to use this principle is in school or other educational situations, but there are many other applications as well. Taking notes in a business meeting and re-forming them into a power point presentation might be one example of this. Use the power of re-forming material into your own words or into a different medium regularly. It is an excellent tool to boost understanding and memorization of any material.

Teach to Remember

A brilliant way to become better at remembering things, and to ensure you fully comprehend them, is to get into the habit of teaching the things you have learnt to other people. When you teach something to another person, you are employing many principles that assist memorization.

First of all, the repetition of the information is, as ever, a helpful aide. By teaching, you are exposing yourself to the material again. By verbalizing it, the material gets ingrained into your mind. And finally, because you have to re-form the material into your own everyday language, you entrench the material still further.

To be able to teach something to another person, you also must comprehend it to a high standard. Teaching is therefore a great test of your understanding. If you haven't learnt the material properly, you won't be able to explain it to someone else. To ensure that you are making complete sense, regularly confirm with whoever you are teaching that they understand what you are saying. Asking them to repeat it back to you can be a final test (and allows them to learn the material through teaching as well).

If you are studying as part of a course, an effective way to implement this principle is to work with a study partner or group. You can then take turns explaining to the other (or the group) what you have learnt. If you divide the work beforehand, you can also save time and spend half as much time (or less) researching and note taking.

Don't Try To Remember Everything
An important principle in improving how you use your memory is learning to rely on your memory at the right times. Recognizing the moments in which you should be using your memory and the times in which it is unnecessary will help save time and energy.

In the modern world, there are many pressures on our attention and many possible inputs for information that we might be expected to remember. However, for many of these, the energy needed to memorize the material is simply not worth it. With numerous tools at our disposal, e.g., pen and paper, calendars, diaries, computers, and smart phones, there is no need to use energy attempting to remember what is not essential. Indeed, whenever it is possible, rely on these things to record information, and only use your memory to remember things of value.

Remembering important dates or when you have appointments is not necessary if you regularly use a calendar. Now, remembering a relative's birthday will prove useful because you will need to know this for the rest of your life. However, is a colleague's birthday worth remembering? Not really. So write it on your calendar. Similarly, remembering your schedule for the coming weeks and months is entirely unnecessary if you own a diary. Don't place unneeded pressure on yourself to remember an appointment next Tuesday at 3PM. Just write it down!

By using the mnemonic techniques you learnt earlier, you could certainly remember these pieces of information if you wanted to. Don't waste time and energy creating a mnemonic device for something that you only need to remember for a few days, especially when recording it in a physical form serves your purposes just as well.

An analogy for this is when cooking a meal. You can try to remember to take the food out of the oven at a certain time, but this will require consistent clock-watching. By setting a timer instead, you can remove the consistent stress of trying to remember, guarantee it is done at the right time, and allow mental space to work on other things.

Other solutions for remembering things with tools include writing down addresses, setting reminders on your phone, saving phone numbers, and writing shopping lists. The rule is: if you only need to remember something for a short time, if it is too valuable to risk forgetting, or if you can record it externally with little effort – record it.

Improve Your Memory by Trusting It

Many people believe that they have a bad memory. This can itself be an obstacle to improving your memory because, by believing this, you will put less conscious effort into remembering things.

A popular phrase is, "I am terrible at remembering people's names." And this is often true; most of us are very bad at remembering names. But when you say it regularly, you will validate the statement and then begin putting little effort into remembering the names of people you meet. By letting yourself off from being good with names, you will end up focusing less on trying to remember, and as we learnt, this focus and effort can be enough in itself to remember names.

If you can cease talking negatively about your memory and realize that you simply haven't yet learnt the skill set, you will have taken a step toward improving how well you memorize things. Everyone can learn how to become good at remembering names, dates, formulas, or anything else. All it takes is application and practice. If you trust your memory, work at using it, and incorporate effective techniques, it will undoubtedly improve.

The Lifestyle to Create a Powerful Mind

Much of the following advice will not be new to you. However, I will reiterate old and new ideas in the hopes of revealing their importance in a new light. They are all essential building blocks to creating a good memory and a powerful mind for life.

1. Get enough sleep.

The human body needs to regenerate, and regularly getting a good night's sleep is essential to creating a lifestyle that enables the mind to grow. Sleep deprivation is a wide-reaching problem in modern society. Too many of us stay up at night watching TV or work too long in the office. Instead, go to bed at the same time every night and try to get the six to eight hours your body and mind need.

2. Enjoy a great diet.

A healthy and balanced diet will perfectly compliment the other steps and create a lifestyle that allows your mind to grow. Eat plenty of fruits and vegetables as well as complete proteins with fatty acids from fish. All of this provides the fuel your mind needs.

Water is also very important. Try to drink 500ml of purified water as soon as you wake up. Throughout the day, don't let yourself get thirsty. As soon as you feel thirsty, your body is already dehydrated and dehydration is one of the biggest physical enemies to focus and memorization.

3. Push your mind.

Studies have shown that one of the most important elements to developing a strong mind is, perhaps obviously, pushing your mind and exerting it regularly.

The careers that we choose perhaps play the biggest role in how we use our minds on a day-to-day. So pursue a career that pushes you mentally (and, of course, a career that you enjoy).

People who work in mentally demanding fields (such as medicine, law, etc.) show greater improvements in IQ over tests performed in their youth than those who work in less demanding roles.

This is perhaps unsurprising, but should not be overlooked. If maintaining a strong and sprightly mind is a priority for you, consider switching to a job role that is mentally challenging and pushes you to memorize material regularly.

4. Remove stress.

This ties in closely with ensuring you get enough sleep. Studies have proven that the ability to think clearly and remember new information is significantly reduced when the individual feels stressed. There are, of course, different kinds of stress. A positive stress that builds focus will helps us to work, and this is to be encouraged. However, consistent, negative, worrying stress should be avoided.

A common form of stress in life is the avoidance of those things that are important. Perhaps we resist looking at our finances, or working at a relationship that isn't working. A powerful way to reduce this kind of stress is to simply address those things we have been avoiding. Easier said than done perhaps, but it depends on how we perceive what is easy. It is surely easier to reduce worry and stress within our life than to live with it.

A great technique for doing this is to set a timer for five minutes and begin to work on what you have been avoiding. Even if it is simply writing in a journal about the issue, this is still a powerful start and will build momentum. Take a break and then work for another five minutes. You will slowly build more energy and find yourself able to work through the issue. Do this for everything you are resisting, and eventually you will significantly reduce stress, letting your mind grow unimpeded.

Section 2 of How to Improve Your Memory and Remember Anything – Flash Cards

Introducing Flash Cards

Flash cards are a study tool that you have no doubt heard of before, indeed probably used at some point in your education. They are especially popular at schools in earlier ages, often used to teach vocabulary to toddlers, also older learners studying another language.

Too often flash cards are pigeonholed and understood to be only good for memorizing simple facts or learning languages word-by-word. However, their application can go much further than this. I will show you how to use flash cards for multiple purposes and how to incorporate them into complete learning systems that will allow you to tackle the greater part of any course you are studying brilliantly well, and with ease.

The Basics: What are Flash Cards?

A flash card is simply a piece of card that has a question on one side and the answer to that question on the other. They are normally small in size, most often found in a 3 x 5 inch form. This is their most popular size, but there is no reason they can't be smaller, perhaps business card sized, or much bigger, perhaps A4 sized or larger. However, the basic format is always the same: a question on one side, and the answer on the other. You can use flash cards both by yourself and with other people.

If you are working alone with a deck of flash cards, the standard process would be to go through the deck card by card, first asking yourself the question, then attempting to answer the question from memory, and finally flipping the card over to see if the answer you gave was correct. Repeat this process with each flash card in the deck.

If two people are participating in studying with flash cards, generally one person will ask questions and the other person will attempt to answer them. Once the answer is given, the person asking the questions will then confirm whether the answer given was correct or not. If the answer given was incorrect, the correct answer on the back of the card must be then conveyed.

The "question" side of the card does not necessarily need to be a fully formed question; it just has to be enough to prompt the appropriate answer from the student. For example, if you were studying the US presidents, specifically when each was born, on one side of the card there might be written: "Abraham Lincoln", and on the other his birth date: "February 12th 1809". And so, if you were using this deck of flash cards by yourself, you would first pick up the card and look only at the "question" side. In this case that would be "Abraham Lincoln." Then you would attempt to recall his birth date. Finally, you would turn over the card and check the answer to see if you were correct.

Flash cards can be used for any subject or topic. They simply contain a chunk of information that needs to be remembered. All that matters is that this chunk is formed into the question and answer format.

The Basics: What to Put on Flash Cards

A flash card can be as detailed or simple as you want it to be. Working with 3 x 5 inch flash cards will encourage you to keep the information brief, and so this is recommended when you are first using flash cards. Keeping information to "bite sized" amounts will make memorization easier, and the entire process of studying with flash cards more manageable, as well as dynamically flexible. In a practical sense, this will also make the cards easier to handle, work with, and carry.

You can also use pictures on your flash cards. An example of this might be if you wanted to learn the names of countries on a map, in which case you would have a map on the "question" side of the card, and then on the opposite side the same map annotated with the correct country names.

If you are learning vocabulary for a new language, you should have the word written in the new language on one side, and then the same word translated into your native language on the other.

Benefits of Flash Cards: Active Recall

Each time you attempt to remember information from a flash card, you are performing "active recall." Active recall is the deliberate attempt to recall a memory. When using a flash card, the question prompts us, and then we attempt to remember the answer from memory.

This contrasts with other actions the mind can engage in, such as when you recall something but not "actively." That is to say, you remember something but didn't try. Instead it just haphazardly entered your conscious mind. For example, if you are walking along a beach, you might recall memories of when you were young and walked on the beach, but the memories in this instance came up without your conscious attempt to recall them.

Active recall also differs from "passive" forms of learning such as reading or listening to a lesson. In these cases the information is simply passing over your mind – being introduced to your mind, rather than being drawn out from within it.

Testing yourself with flash cards utilizes active recall repeatedly, because with every flash card you attempt to answer the question it asks. But why is active recall so important?

When you attempt to actively recall something and answer a question on a flash card, there are a few things that happen. If you answer the question correctly, the act of recalling the information will solidify the memory into your mind. Recalling it actively means this memory will now live on in your mind for longer than it would have if you hadn't attempted to recall it again. It is impossible to say when the memory would have left you, maybe a day later or a week later, there is no way to know. But one thing is for sure: memories will deteriorate if they are not strengthened, and recalling them actively is an excellent way to strengthen them.

Using flash cards and applying spaced interval systems (we'll get to those soon) that apply adaptive testing will ensure that the memory is further strengthened if it needs to be, and less so if it doesn't. Using flash cards means that you utilize active recall and enjoy the benefits of using it to powerfully and dependably improve the memorization of material.

Benefits of Flash Cards: Adaptive Self-Testing

Another strength of using flash cards is that it is a form of testing, and if you use them by yourself, it is a form of self-testing. The benefits of testing are numerous, and perhaps obvious, nonetheless I want to take a moment to exemplify the benefits.

Testing with flash cards will give you an accurate reflection of how well you actually know a subject, as the information has been divided down into small chunks that fit on 3x5 inch cards. Once you have been tested, you know exactly what parts you know and what sections need improvement.

When using flash cards, there is little room to misinterpret how well you know a subject. There is no way to sugar coat how well you are doing. You will find out exactly how close you are to total comprehension of a given topic. Additionally, if you made the flash cards so they rigorously follow the course syllabus, you will be able to accurately predict how well you will do when you sit the exam.

Knowing how well you are doing in your course, and how much work you still need to do, will help you develop confidence if you are doing well, and/or apply realistic and accurate pressure to work on areas you are struggling with.

One of the main obstacles to good studying is being unaware of what needs to be learnt: students too easily confuse what needs to be learnt with what doesn't. Regular testing is the only way to solve this, and flash cards provide this solution elegantly well.

The flexible testing system of flash cards also means that you study the things you need to study and nothing more. In this manner you prevent yourself from re-addressing things you have already learnt and from spending too little time on what you still need to learn. This is a vital strength of flash cards. This reason alone makes them exceptionally useful study tools.

Developing your ability to understand how well you are learning and how best to improve your study techniques is a strong part of becoming an effective student. Through creating your own study systems with flash cards, you can always get an accurate representation of where you are at as well as what needs to be done to get the grades you want.

Benefits of Flash Cards: Simple Format, Many Applications

Creating and using flash cards is an exceptionally easy, straightforward process. It can take time to master their more complex applications, but to use them in a basic manner is easy. A flash card can be as simple as a picture of a cat on one side and the word "cat" on the other. The memorization process can begin with something as simple as this.

Flash cards are therefore applicable to any level of learning. Anything that needs to be remembered can be presented in the flash card format, making them very flexible in this respect.

Another reason to consider incorporating flash cards into your study skill set is that they can be used in a variety of ways. If you are a teacher, providing a few flash cards to a child or group is straightforward and allows them to teach themselves whilst monitoring their own progress. Flash cards might also be used by a medical student to help break down a course into manageable chunks. By developing and utilizing a good study system, he or she can effectively work through flash cards whilst the system adapts to how well he or she is memorizing the material, by increasing or diminishing exposure as needed.

Benefits of Flash Cards: Break Topics into Manageable Chunks

Creating your own flash cards for a course is a fantastic way to break up what you are studying and make it more manageable.

Feeling overwhelmed with too much information and not knowing where to start is a common problem that students face. If you leave material untouched for too long or miss a few classes, you are likely to find yourself presented with a stack of information without there being any clear place to begin.

Creating one flash card at a time is a simple but powerful act that forces you to create bite-sized chunks of information and to compartmentalize what may otherwise be extended and complex ideas, morphing it into something more manageable. Using flash cards that are only 3 x 5 inches can be a great way to force you to keep these chunks of information to a small size so that they can be memorized without excessive effort.

The act of studying with flash cards is also modular in a more general sense. Working with decks of flash cards that correspond to topics and subtopics means you can pick areas to work on easily. It is wise to encourage this practice by using different colors to denote certain topics. Making it clear which flash card is for which subject area re-affirms that there are clear divisions in your work. Even if these divisions and subtopics are at times arbitrary (perhaps you are dividing decks based solely on page numbers in your text book), ensuring that you keep things sectioned will prevent the flash cards, and the study process as a whole, from becoming overwhelming.

Benefits of Flash Cards: Think and Work in Questions and Answers

Another reason that working with flash cards is so effective is because they force you to think in terms of questions and answers.

Turning every element of your course into small questions and answers is a powerful study tool in itself. It pushes you to re-form all the information into the question/answer format, forcing a deeper understanding and initializing memorization immediately.

Let's now look at how to create and use flash cards in more detail.

Making Flash Cards vs. Buying Flash Cards

When using physical flash cards, you have the choice of either purchasing readymade ones or making your own. There are advantages for each, which we will cover now. More often than not, however, I would encourage you to make your own, for reasons I will make clear.

Purchasing flash cards is exceptionally easy, and saves time and effort. If you go online, it is easy to find quality flash cards simply by searching "flash cards" on Amazon or eBay alongside the topic you are studying. In most cases there will be decks of cards, often at very reasonable prices. For the sake of ease, buying flash cards ready-to-use is unbeatable. If the thought of making your own is too daunting and you just want an easy introduction to flash cards, purchasing them is advisable. It can also save you a lot of time to purchase them online and have them delivered to your home. So if you are drawing close to a deadline and need flash cards as soon as possible, don't hesitate to buy them!

However, if you do have the time, it can be much better to make your own flashcards. First of all, it will be cheaper to buy cards and pens rather than purchasing readymade flash cards. For cash-strapped university students in particular, creating your own flash cards will be kind to overstretched bank accounts.

Making your own flash cards should also guarantee good quality. When purchasing flash cards online, there is always a risk that either the physical quality or the way the flash cards are written will not be up to par. However, by making your own flash cards, you can take the time needed to produce quality flash cards.

By creating your own flash cards, you can also be absolutely sure that everything you need to know is on the flash cards – nothing more and nothing less. Unless you buy flash cards from the specific exam board you are studying for, there is little chance that purchased flash cards will be a complete match for what you need to learn for a specific exam. Similarly, if you do decide to buy flash cards, check thoroughly that the ones you buy are as close a match as possible to the course you are studying.

Studying flash cards that contain unneeded information is a waste of your time. Even worse, if the cards do not cover necessary material, you will compromise your exam performance and final grade. Of course, if you are studying a language or are studying for pleasure, there is no risk here. However, if you are studying for an exam, using a deck of flash cards that dovetails as completely as possible with the syllabus is a must.

Make Flash Cards Visually Striking

Flash cards come in many forms, but their simplest look is black text on white paper. There is nothing wrong with this, but there are many occasions in which including pictures and other visuals will help your studies. Even when you are using flash cards to learn rote facts, creating visually striking cards is a fantastic idea because it will improve your study experience. Let's now look at how you can create more visual impact with your flash cards.

The simplest manner to create visually striking flash cards is to incorporate pictures. If you are studying biology and need to learn the different parts of the leaf, you could draw a cross-section of a leaf on the "question" side with five blank boxes beside the parts you need to name. Then, on the other side, include the same image with the correct answers written in the boxes.

Taking time to draw images when creating flash cards can also be a good way to add some variety to studying.

If you are predominantly a visual learner and remember images well, embrace using images as much as possible because you will find these easier to memorize than just facts and ideas. Working in tune with your preferred learning style will make your studies more fruitful and rewarding.

Varying the color of ink you write in is another way to make flash cards more effective. If you are learning sentences in a new language, you can use different colors for nouns, verbs, adjectives, etc. If you are a visual learner and are learning facts, just "words on the page," write in different colors. Then when you are initially learning the answer or are correcting yourself, take a few moments to look at the card and take in the aesthetic. This will stick in your mind more powerfully than just black words on white paper.

Another way to use different colors when writing text on a flash card is to break up different parts of the word and write them in different colors. For example, if you are studying chemistry you may come across a long word that can be broken into separate parts – parts that point to the origin of the entire word. In such a case you can use a different color for each part of the word, then on the answer side, break down the ontology of the word with its corresponding color/parts. For instance, the word "photosynthesis" could be broken into two parts: "photo" and "synthesis". Write these two parts in different colors, then on the answer side write: "photo = light" and "synthesis = putting together". You may choose to include a full definition of photosynthesis as well. Writing in different colors will make a stronger impression on the mind and help you to more clearly remember the root meanings of the word, as well as the full definition of photosynthesis.

Making the flash card itself a certain color can also help you to get the most out of your study experience. Using cards of different colors will help you to group the cards into different topics. If you make different decks different colors, not only will they be easier to work with, they will also help memorization as the set color for each deck will help your mind to associate the information together more effectively. The mind works through association, and the simple act of keeping topics linked by a certain color will help you to link the same facts and ideas together in your mind, improving memorization.

Practical Tips for Creating Flash Cards

If you are making your own flash cards, there are a few things to bear in mind in order to make them as practical and effective as possible.

Laminating your flash cards to protect them and make them more durable is a great idea – unless you are only going to use them a few times (and have created them perhaps a week before an exam), in which case there is no need to go through the effort. However, if you are going to use the cards multiple times, laminating them will ensure they survive being used many times, as well as being thrown in a bag or being studied in the rain whilst waiting for a bus.

Endeavor to always make flash cards out of card as well. Using paper flash cards will often result in the ink running through or being seen on the other side, which will obviously ruin any testing experience. Card is also just easier to handle and will make the flash cards more durable.

You may find it easier to make your flash cards on a computer. It is easy to create flash cards in Word or Excel. Simply create a large symmetrical table and then cut it out once you have printed it. Doing so will often be easier and more practical because you can more easily copy and paste pictures and repeat similar cards.

However, it will help the learning process if you write on the cards and draw pictures yourself. Doing this is a more tactile and memorable experience that will help you to remember the information.

If you are working with children, making flash cards larger than 3 x 5 inches is a great idea because it makes them both easier and a little more fun to use.

Many stationary departments will sell decks of blank flash cards. These can be very useful as cutting out small cards to the correct size is time-consuming. The nominal cost will be worth it. If you purchase blank card decks, they may come with their own small box, but if not, most stationary stores will sell small boxes (certainly A5 size) that will make storing and transporting the flash cards easier. If not, small pencil cases or even elastic bands can be excellent for holding a deck of flash cards together.

It is also helpful to ensure that your flash card decks stay separate. It can be difficult and time-consuming to separate flash cards back into their respective topics. Always keeping flash cards as modular, separate decks will make study sessions simpler to arrange and implement. When you are planning and executing your study sessions, make them as dedicated and clear cut as possible, for example, "study flash card deck B on organic chemistry."

What to Do When Questions are Answered Incorrectly

When working with flash cards, you will be consistently asking yourself or someone else a question. When you (or they) give a correct answer, simply confirm that the answer given was correct and move on to the next card. However, when an incorrect answer is given, what to do next is not so clear-cut. There are a few options that can significantly affect whether the information will be remembered the next time.

There should always be exposure to the correct answer. Little progress will be made if whoever is being tested is not informed of the correct answer and given a chance to re-affirm the memory. (There may be odd exceptions to this rule, for example, if you are doing a quiz). If you are working with a system (which I will explain later in detail), the card must be moved to a stage where there will be re-exposure sooner rather than later. This is essential.

If you are working by yourself and give an incorrect answer, you can simply read the answer to yourself (doing it aloud will be more beneficial) to re-form the memory of the correct answer. Once you have read the correct answer, it may help to then ask yourself the question again and repeat the answer from memory. Doing this once or twice as a practice may be helpful, but attempt to do so quickly. Moving through a deck at a prompt, consistent pace is desirable.

What you do in response to a wrong answer might also depend on how far from the answer you were. If you were very close, simply re-reading the answer once aloud will be enough. If your answer was completely incorrect, re-test yourself a couple of times. Obviously your study goals affect how you should react to a wrong answer, so if you need to remember this card by tomorrow, consider continued testing until you recall it from memory easily.

If you are working with someone else, there are various options you can experiment with. You can ask them to try again if they were close to the answer, or perhaps give hints. Both of these are often preferable to just saying "wrong" and moving on. Offering hints will allow the individual to engage intellectually and will strengthen a weak memory more effectively, rather than simple re-exposure to the correct answer.

It is usually beneficial to be consistent when responding to incorrect answers with yourself to ensure you are never lenient and that you move through work briskly. However, if you are a teacher or parent working with a child, be as flexible as you feel will be helpful and supportive.

Dealing with Repeated Incorrect Answers

You may occasionally get stuck attempting to remember a flash card. No matter how hard you try, you just can't remember the answer. As a result (if you are working with a "system"), you will be exposed to the flash card more often. But what should you do when even then you fail to remember the correct answer?

If you are experiencing this problem with one or multiple cards, you have a few options. You can...

- Make the flash card easier. Perhaps the information is too hard and you need to make it simpler to memorize.
- Reduce the amount of information on the flash card. There may be too much for you to remember as it is. Breaking it up so that the information fits onto two or maybe three flash cards, rather than just one, will improve your chances of memorization and consequently correct answers on testing.
- Increase the frequency of exposure. Perhaps at present you are leaving too much time between periods of testing, and so the memory of the answer has faded out by the time you come to test yourself again. Lessen the possibility of wrong answers by increasing the frequency of testing (this is especially advisable if there are multiple cards in the deck you are really struggling with).
- Alter/improve how you act when you get a question incorrect. Perhaps you are too passive in attempting to establish the information even as a short-term memory. Try reading it aloud, re-testing the card straight away, or writing down the answer.
- You can also utilize mnemonic tricks to make memorization easier. If you are attempting to memorize a formula, perhaps turn the letters into the initials of a memorable sentence or transform the information by associating it with things/animals/people, turning the

formula into an interesting and dynamic visual scene. This will stick in your memory more than drab, grey ideas. For more mnemonic ideas, search online for free lessons on sites such as YouTube.

Use Multiple Decks

Creating multiple decks of flash cards will make studying easier because you can compartmentalize your course more clearly. If you use just one deck of flash cards and continually add to it, at some point it will become difficult to manage, both physically and in terms of creating flexible study schedules in which you cover a whole deck of cards in a session.

There are no definite rules, but the deck will become tougher to work with when it becomes larger than fifty cards. At this point it is wise to break the deck into separate topics. Also, when the deck gets too big you risk not gaining enough exposure to all the flash cards. Finally, decks too large are to be avoided because they are more daunting to begin studying, which may cause you to procrastinate.

Before you create your flash cards, it is best to decide on the topics and subtopics you are going to divide your course into, and then create decks that are of a reasonable and uniform size. This will make scheduling and implementing study periods with the flash cards much easier.

It can also be a good idea to predetermine which decks are more important than others and to prioritize the essential decks. You can then study the important decks more regularly than others, and the decks that carry extraneous information can be circulated into your study sessions less regularly. Be aware, however, that working like this can become a little complex. I would recommend that beginners create flash card decks of the same "value." There are no definite rules, so experiment and find what works best for you.

Create Decks that Rigorously Follow your Course

To make studying with flash cards as effective as possible, the flash cards you use must rigorously adhere to the course you are studying. If you create flash cards that contain information that you won't be tested on, you will be wasting time. If you don't include what you will be tested on, you will lose marks before you even walk into the exam hall.

If you are working toward exam success and the highest grade possible, the best way for you to create a flash card deck that comprehensively follows the course is to create flash cards from previous exam papers. First, check with your teacher to ensure the exam won't deviate much from previous years. If it won't, find exam papers from the last few years, perhaps the last five, and from these create flash cards that allow you to answer these past exam papers brilliantly well.

If the above is not possible, do your best to find material that comes closest to the course syllabus. You can also ask your teacher where you can find questions that may come up in the exam or ask him/her to compose questions you can work from.

If you want to enjoy the material and expand your understanding beyond what you are going to be tested on, then absolutely make your flash cards more expansive. This is particularly wise if the subject you are studying is part of a field you are going to work in professionally for years to come. In this case the more groundwork and depth to the knowledge you build, the better.

Flash Cards as Part of the Learning Process

Another reason to make your own flash cards is that you can use the process of creating them a strong part of the learning process. To create flash cards for your course, you need to first find the vital ingredients that will be on the exam, then condense them into your own words, and finally, re-form them into small, testable pieces.

This short series of steps will often, in itself, be enough exposure to the course material for memorization (at least in the short-term). Following this with testing yourself or others will cement the information into your long-term memory. You should also use other flash card techniques to create a breadth and depth to your studying – techniques that will build deeper understanding and establish how all the elements of the course interact with one another.

The process of condensing information down by choosing what is vital to be learnt, posing it into questions and answers, and neatly mounting these onto small cards is a series of learning moments. These act as an excellent segue into the adaptive testing systems and active recall moments which can facilitate complete memorization of your course.

Of course there are many other forms of study that could constitute the initial exposure to information. It could be note taking in class, reading a text book, or listening to an audio recording. There are many possibilities, but regardless of which act precedes testing with flash cards, I would encourage you to make sure that you have learnt the information at least fairly well. If you move to testing with flash cards and most of your answers are incorrect, you did not learn the information at all, and the initial flash card test (and perhaps subsequent ones) will be a waste of time. If you then choose to continue without another mode of study, you will be relying on the method of correction you are using following incorrect flash card answers.

Flash cards can be the initial study approach if applied properly. Whatever the first learning process is, ensure that it is fairly successful, otherwise the initial flash card tests will be a waste of time, and you will be putting a large amount of faith in the correction process you are using.

Note Taking with Flash Cards

Note taking involves recording information and compressing a large amount of content down to a condensed summary. By creating flash cards, you are performing this process to re-form everything into questions and answers. Therefore, it is possible to replace the conventional forms of note taking you use and instead create flash cards. Consider adding the creation of flash cards to your note taking tool box.

Creating flash cards directly from the source can be a good approach if you are confident with the course already, or if you are on a tight deadline. Constructing flash cards directly from the course material will remove what are often unnecessary intermediary steps. You are immediately creating the means by which you will memorize and test yourself on the material.

It will often be possible to create flash cards directly from a lesson. So instead of taking notes in the manner you normally do, simply convert the information you hear directly into the flash card format.

Arrive to class with a deck of blank 3 x 5 flash cards, and then as you hear important ideas and snippets of information you think will be necessary to learn, record these on one side of the flash cards. Put the appropriate question on the other side that would prompt the answer. Perhaps write in pencil at first and then revise them at home, tracing over them in pen if you feel they are accurate and useful.

It is important that you create accurate flash cards. If you feel the accuracy of the flash cards is not what it should be, don't incorporate them into the testing system you are using. It may be a good idea to have a teacher or successful colleague evaluate whether they are an accurate representation of the class.

Taking notes like this may take time to master, and is perhaps best suited to classes in which there is little risk of you falling behind, as this task requires a higher level of concentration. However, if you can master this skill, you will save a lot of time and effort. This is because once you have created the flash cards, you can effectively use them exclusively to learn the course material.

A note taking skill that can always be applied with flash cards is to take notes from already assembled information. If you have a collection of articles or book extracts and want to condense them down to a workable form – differentiating the unimportant from the important – creating flash cards can be an easy and effective approach.

Expanding Understanding with Flash Cards

Flash cards are best known for learning facts or vocabulary, but they can also be used to develop understanding of deeper concepts and to build depth and breadth of knowledge.

An example of a flash card used to develop understanding could have on the question side: "State three reasons the North won the American Civil War." This is not as two-dimensional or "black and white" as the question found on the conventional flash card. It expands into deeper territory, and consequently, giving a definitive "yes" or "no" is not possible. There are also more than three possible reasons the North won the Civil War, so there must be previous experience of the three reasons given on the reverse of this specific flash card. It would be unfair and unwise to use such a flash card for the first time on a fellow history student. It would only be effective if they had learnt the three reasons specifically on the reverse of this flash card.

Using flash cards in this way is very effective. You can use the same kind of understanding based questions that might appear on an exam, and use flash cards to build on understanding as well as knowledge. If you are studying subjects such as English literature or history, flash cards can be helpful in memorizing deeper ideas and developing and solidifying understanding. Indeed, subjects like these (even at higher levels) can be studied effectively and, if desired, almost exclusively with flash cards.

It will be more difficult to test when using flash cards in this manner. It will not always be as straightforward as when learning rote facts and vocabulary. It will require you to decide how close you, or the person you are testing, came to the correct answer. Try to err on the side of being too strict to avoid incomplete learning, but also do not only accept word-for-word answers because this will be a waste of time and not be reflective of true learning.

When deciding on whether the answer given is correct or not, look for accurate paraphrasing as well as the presence of key words. It may be helpful to underline key words beforehand in order to be clear about which words must be in a possible answer. This will keep the testing more accurate without being unfeasibly rigorous.

Flash cards are predominantly known for learning key facts and ideas, but there is no reason not to expand their use in order to teach yourself, and others, a deeper understanding of a given topic. Testing may be more difficult, but do not let this discourage you. In time you will develop an accurate ability to mark yourself and others.

Establish Connections and Relationships

Another fantastic use for flash cards is to assist in building your understanding of relationships. Flash cards are easy to manipulate and move around physically; therefore, you can establish relationships in a clear visual sense by rearranging them on a table.

First, decide what kind of relationships you will attempt to establish. If you are working on your knowledge of US presidents, first turn all the cards so they are on a surface with the president's names showing face up. There are then many ways you can manipulate the cards to develop your understanding of the subject. Perhaps if you are currently studying the historical differences between the Democratic and Republican parties, you could move the flash cards into two groups: Republican presidents on the right and Democrat presidents on the left. The simple act of moving them into position will help you to establish the connections, and the visual of presenting them in this way will help you to remember which president was part of which party.

Once you have established which party each respective president was a part of, you might then continue to develop your understanding by putting them in chronological order as well. Or you might order them by the length of term they served in office.

These are a few simple examples, but there are many ways to manipulate flash cards to establish connections. Another example would be if you were working with the elements of the periodic table. You could place the elements in groups according to which ones react in a similar manner when added to a certain chemical. There are many possibilities, so be creative.

Working with flash cards in this way embraces different modes of thinking. The tactile and visual dynamic of working with flash cards helps to build connections more organically. Be creative and build your understanding of the relationships that exist within a topic by using flash cards in this manner.

Flash Cards with Others: An Introduction

Flash cards are a brilliant way to facilitate people learning together. There are various study techniques and games that can be played with two or more people. All these study methods utilize flash cards and can make learning more effective, social, and fun.

Making flash cards as a part of a study group can be a great way for you to learn and work together. Working in this way helps you to bounce ideas off one another, identifying and establishing the key parts of the course. It is also a great way for a study group to pool notes from class, which can be followed by consolidation of the information down to the most important.

A study group might also work together to make a deck that contains the vocabulary and key terms from a course. This is easiest to do by working from a glossary of terms in a textbook.

If you are a teacher, or in charge of the learning of others, there are many ways to facilitate greater variation in learning by using flash cards. By providing a deck of flash cards to a group, you give them an excellent opportunity to work unassisted as well as to develop their interpersonal/team building skills. With children especially, the introduction of flash cards will help them improve and regulate their own learning, as well as the learning of their classmates.

Flash Cards with Others: Having Fun

Creating a quiz from flash cards is a very straightforward way to have fun with classmates, while still learning. To do this, simply divide the group into two, and then ask questions from a deck of flash cards. The more fun you can make the quiz, the better – so try to include prizes and perhaps give each team something to signal with when they know the answer, like a bell or a whistle.

This technique may seem elementary or childish, but proves to be both enjoyable and effective for all ages – even university students and adults in a professional setting.

Another game to play with flash cards is to put an entire deck of cards in a bag and then ask whomever you are studying with to reach in and fish out a card to answer. This will again make simple testing routines more interesting, especially for children, who will enjoy the novelty of the game.

With a group you can also play a game of "musical flash cards." To play this game, sit in a circle, and then pass around a deck of flash cards whilst music plays. Stop the music at random, and whoever is holding the deck when the music stops, must answer the top flash card. Again, make it interesting by adding a prize. Perhaps sweets or maybe an early exit from class.

Because flash cards are a form of testing, they serve as a helpful tool for a teacher to assess how well a class is doing. On top of this, flash cards offer a great deal of flexibility and can be adapted into a variety of games that ensure the class has fun and stays engaged.

One-Sided Flash Cards

Flash cards do not always have to be two-sided. One-sided flash cards can be used to utilize different study techniques. Using flash cards in this way will mean that you need two packs: one for answers and one for questions. You will need a way to remember which are linked, that is to say, which questions correspond to which answers. Perhaps create a table that states all the paired questions and answers.

Once you have made your one-sided flash cards, you can use games and systems that are specific to one-sided flash cards. For example, a simple game of "pairs" will encourage your learning if you enjoy visual games, and can be played by yourself or with others. To play, take turns flipping over two of the cards, then attempt to remember where the "pairs" are, i.e., the corresponding question and answer cards. Eventually, you will endeavor to turn them both over on the same go. If you match a corresponding pair, you get another turn. Each time you match a pair you get one point, and whoever has the most points once all the pairs have been matched is declared the winner.

Of course, be sure that you are correctly pairing the questions with the right answers. This game is best played when a fairly strong understanding of the flash cards has already been developed and only revision is needed.

Studying with a System: Introducing Adaptive Testing

If you are using a deck of flash cards on your own, I highly recommend that you employ some type of "system" that dictates when you re-test yourself on each respective card. Studying with flash cards in this way means that you will be utilizing the effects of "spaced exposure," which means you are exposed to the information you need to memorize repeatedly and over a long period of time.

Spaced exposure contrasts with "mass" exposure. Mass exposure occurs when you attempt to learn many things by repeated exposure over a short amount of time. Mass exposure is often referred to as "cramming," which is a popular study approach for many students (normally because they procrastinated until days before the exam), and although it is conventionally seen as unwise, cramming does have its merits. Cramming does facilitate good retention into the short-term memory, but there is only a limited amount of information you can "cram" into your mind and retain in the short-term memory space. In order to memorize enough information to achieve a high grade in a course, there must be deposits into the long-term memory. In order to create real understanding and to take in information at depth, spaced exposure is also by far the superior method of learning.

Utilizing a system with flash cards ensures you correctly expose yourself to the material and use "active recall" to study at spaced intervals. The system will dictate the time interval between testing on a given flash card. Every system is designed to expose you more frequently to information you are yet to correctly memorize and less frequently to information you have already memorized.

A good system will ensure that you come as close as possible to testing yourself with the flash cards at the "right" time. By this I mean you test yourself regularly enough, but no more than necessary. So that when you come to the exam, you have them ingrained in your mind, and recollection of the information is easy. The goal is to test yourself on a flash card before the date that you would have forgotten the answer is, but as close to that date as possible so that you don't waste time testing yourself more than necessary.

There is no perfect way to expose yourself to material so that you aren't exposed to it more than necessary (or too little). There can only be best guesses and nominalized systems that create the best possible fit. Regardless, be sure to use a system for learning from flash cards. Doing so will mean you use your study time significantly more effectively.

Studying with a System: An Example of a Simple System

I will now explain a simple example of a testing system you can use with flash cards. I recommend attempting to implement this system first so that you establish an understanding of the basic principles.

The simplest form a learning system can take on is to move the flash card to the back of the deck if it is answered correctly, and move it to the middle of the deck if you answered it incorrectly. Continue working through the deck from front to back. Working in this way, you will be continually exposed to those questions you have answered incorrectly, before you return to those that you have answered correctly. This ensures that you study (through active recall) the material you have yet to memorize. It will make it easier if you place a divider half way through the deck, and then place all incorrectly answered flash cards just in front of that divider.

This is the simplest method that embraces the spaced exposure approach, and by itself it can be very effective. Its strength is in being straightforward and easy to apply. So if you are new to flash cards and in a hurry to start using them, I recommend trying this method out first. Within perhaps an hour of working with them, you will be able to see how much more effective your studying is when you consistently tackle your weakest areas.

If the above system suits your goals and works well for you, stick with it. As with many things, what is simple is often best.

Studying with a System: Implementing the "Leitner" System

The "Leitner System" is slightly more advanced in how it applies the spaced exposure principle. This is a very flexible system that can be adapted to a variety of courses and study goals. Here is an example of how it can work:

There are five stages each flash card goes through. Each time you actively recall an answer successfully, the flash card gets moved up a stage. Each time you get it wrong, the flash card will move back down a stage.

It can be helpful to use five boxes or pencil cases – anything to help physically differentiate between each stage.

When a card is answered correctly, it goes up a stage, i.e., from stage 1 to stage 2. When a card is answered incorrectly, it goes down a stage, i.e., from stage 2 to stage 1. The stage a card is at dictates when it will be reviewed. In this example:

Stage 1 is reviewed daily

Stage 2 is reviewed once a week

Stage 3 twice a month

Stage 4 once a month

Stage 5 every three months

During your first session with the flash cards, each will begin at stage 1. Following the initial test, each correctly answered card will be promoted to stage 2. Each incorrectly answered card remains at stage 1.

The following day you will work through stage 1 again (cards at this stage are reviewed every day) and test yourself on all the cards you answered incorrectly the day before, whereas the flash cards you answered correctly the previous day will not be reviewed until the following week, on whatever day you designate for your stage 2 reviews (perhaps this is every Monday).

It is important to keep the once a week reviews on the same day, e.g., every Monday, so that you can build the habit and ensure optimal testing. If you leave it until Wednesday and nine days pass between testing, you may lose some information, and flash cards that would have been committed to memory won't be.

This process continues in the same manner: each day you review cards at stage 1 and then the next (and every) Monday you work through the stage 2 cards. When you work through the stage 2 cards, those that are answered correctly are promoted to stage 3 and will be reviewed every month (again, pick a day and stick to it). Those answered incorrectly are demoted to stage 1, and will therefore be reviewed the following day, and daily, until you answer them correctly and they return to stage 2. And so on, and so forth...

You can be as flexible as you want in your application of the Leitner System. The "stages" can be over any time frame you see fit. Also, there doesn't have to be five stages – there can be as many as you want – though don't use too many as this will become increasingly difficult to manage.

For a test that is a year away, the above example is an excellent application of the Leitner System. The daily review stage will mean competence is reached quickly, and by incorporating the fifth and final stage (which gets reviewed every 3 months) you will ensure that you retain the information long-term, without excessive exposure.

Studying with a System: A "Total" Study System

In order to become an effective student of whatever you are studying, it can be very helpful to work with a structured system. Using the Leitner System, in some form, will allow you to develop a regular protocol for remembering necessary information. I will now provide further advice so that you can create a "total" system. This will combine all methods to create an ideal studying experience.

In order to facilitate continued learning of a whole subject, it is advisable to slowly introduce more flash cards to the system (always beginning new flash cards at stage 1). As flash cards are promoted through the stages, and you memorize the course material, introduce more flash cards to the process. Attempt to balance the speed at which cards are being promoted with the speed at which you introduce them. If you need to learn at a faster rate than you are, you will need more review sessions. You could perhaps make stage 1 a twice daily review and stage 2 a daily review, thus allowing you to learn faster and get through more new material.

Create and work a system that specifically caters to you and your study goals. However, do not attempt to take on too many study sessions too soon. The habit of studying itself will be difficult to instill, and attempting to memorize too much material will cause you to struggle to learn as effectively.

Creating a regular pattern to your flash card system is very important. The more habitual and repetitive you can make the system, the easier you will find it to implement, and the more energy you can devote to actually studying the cards.

Introducing flash cards at a regular rate is an important element. A sustainable rate, i.e., where flash cards move up stages roughly as fast as they are introduced, is most desirable.

To begin using a system, you need to establish the rate at which you need to introduce new information. In order to do this, you must be aware of the total amount of information you need to memorize. Ideally, do this by knowing how many flash cards worth of information your course constitutes. You also need to know the date by which the information must be memorized. Then you can create a Leitner-esque system which will bring about enough exposure to the collection of flash cards by that date.

Make it regular and easily habituated by introducing a new flash card each day for each sub-topic you are learning. This will help to make the process easily practiced and maintained. Working like this requires you to diligently dissect the course material so that cards can be introduced at the rate of one card per day. If you are yet to receive all the information needed for the exam, this will be very much an estimation at first. But don't worry about this. It is far better to have a structured approach to learning the course, even if the structure of the approach is based on educated guesses.

The more you can nominalize and create rigorous learning systems, the better you will be able to study and absorb information. The act of learning one thing per day will allow your memory to adapt into a pattern of learning. The ability to recall information will slowly improve as you work every day. Like a muscle gaining strength through regular exertion.

Using Flash Card Software

Using software that embraces the flash card principles is also recommended. Although you will not get the same tactile experience that can be so beneficial for some learners, there are nonetheless many advantages to using flash card software.

There are a few great flash card websites that a quick Google search will reveal. They all work in a similar way, with slight differences in the systems they utilize (as in the Leitner System, etc.). Experiment with using the top few options. Each will have different benefits that dovetail to varying degrees with your learning goals.

A tremendous benefit of using software is that there are already databases full of flash cards ready for you to use, and since they are digital, you can easily search and find many decks of flash cards. For more popular subjects, and language learning in particular, there will be all the flash cards you need waiting for you online.

There are also apps you can download to use on your smart phone or tablet. This, again, makes the flash card process something you can utilize at any time. Running through a deck of flash cards on your phone is even easier as you don't need to remember to bring additional items with you.

There are several strengths to using flash card software, and I would encourage you to take a few hours to experiment with the available software. However, as a day-to-day study tool, it is much better to make your own physical flash cards since you can then be confident that you are studying the proper information. On top of this, you encourage the learning process through the act of creating the flash cards themselves.

BONUS SECTION: HOW TO STUDY

Introduction

The aim of this book is to give you tips to make your time studying as successful and enjoyable as possible. It contains my best advice on time management, goal setting, and how to get the best grades with the least effort. It's advice that also transfers brilliantly well to professionals, the self-employed, and anyone who manages their own projects and/or daily work cycle.

(If you fall into the non-student category, whenever you see the word "study" throughout this book, think the word "work" instead, and whenever you see "grades" think "work goals".)

There's nothing more to say, so let's get started!

Build the Study Habit and Schedule Study Times

One of the main reasons students don't get good grades is simple: they don't have the study habit. Being able to regularly make yourself sit down and learn the necessary material is an essential part of becoming a great student.

Both when you study and the length of time you study for should be as regular and routine as possible. This will make the habit of studying easier to begin and sustain over time. Working at the same time every day is the best way to do this, e.g., between 7 and 9 every morning. (This time works well as it is before classes.) Of course, your study time will depend on the courses you are taking and your other commitments.

Working at set times every day will help build the habit of studying. There will be less urge to procrastinate and do unimportant tasks because you know when you should be working and when you shouldn't. Eventually it will actually take more willpower not to study at these times because you will subconsciously expect to be utilizing your study time.

Time Box Tasks

To build a sense of urgency and avoid being overwhelmed with work, it is helpful to create definite periods of time or 'time boxes' in which you work.

Set a timer and do not work for more or less than the time you set. Then, take a break for a small timed period. Rinse and repeat. Working like this will help you overcome procrastination because you will not feel the sense of being overwhelmed by a project. One of the main reasons that students (or anyone) procrastinate is that they feel anxious about not knowing how to begin and/or that they will have to keep working for a long time. By limiting the time spent working on something to a set number, we can alleviate anxiety caused by either of these problems.

Working for a definite amount of time also helps stop perfectionism and curbs the desire to spend more time on a project than is necessary. Many people suffer from this. They work long hours to make their project as perfect as it can possibly be. Sometimes this leads to people doing great things. However, it is more often an enemy of productivity as it leads to a task dragging on for longer than needed. For example, if it takes 10 hours to complete an assignment to a 70 percent standard, is it worth working 20 hours to complete it to a 72 percent standard? Sometimes yes, but usually no. Time boxing is an excellent tool for stopping perfectionism in its tracks. It forces us to complete a task to a good standard and no more.

Both for study sessions and for whole projects, many students find they work more effectively by working to a time scale. In doing so, you will create a greater sense of urgency to your work, as you only think about continuing work until the timer sounds. The alternative of working for an unspecified amount of time makes both beginning and continuing work more difficult. It also encourages a slow, non-urgent work mode and/or perfectionism. To avoid this, use time boxing and set time limits for your work.

Prioritize Assignments and Be Aware of Grade Boundaries/Percentages

The extent to which a project affects your grade and how long it takes to complete will vary in relation to one another. Therefore, it is important to spend more time on those projects that contribute more marks and less on those that don't.

At the beginning of the academic year, you should deconstruct your course so that you know what percentage each module/exam/project will contribute toward the final grade. This will reveal which areas require more time and effort than others. It will often not be clear what the more valuable modules are until you do this.

You can then place more emphasis on the areas that contribute more to your overall grade and limit time spent on the less valuable. Re-adjust where you are placing your time and effort as you receive feedback throughout the year. Be flexible and note where you are struggling to get the grades you want. When you receive marks for coursework, rework these into your plans. For example, if you do very well in a piece of coursework, scale back the time you planned to spend revising for its corresponding exam, and instead, prepare for an exam on a topic you are struggling with. There is no way to perfectly balance this, as it will be based on guesswork. Simply do your best, and work as intelligently as you can.

Test Yourself Frequently

Always being aware of exactly how well you are progressing toward your final grade is essential in order to adjust your study plans and better understand what you need to work on. Apart from coursework and feedback in class, testing yourself is the best way to do this.

Gather past exam papers/questions and frequently test yourself with them. Ideally, use entire test papers from previous years (assuming the course hasn't changed too drastically). Also, test yourself in conditions similar to how you will take the actual exam. Giving yourself the same amount of time as you will get in the real exam is crucial. Set a timer and stick to it. Once you have completed the exam paper, mark it yourself or give it to a teacher/lecturer/fellow student to mark. Make sure whoever is marking it does so by following a correct answer sheet/mark scheme.

Ascertaining what level you are currently working at will reveal where your subsequent studies should concentrate. For example, if you are working on an essay-based exam, you might learn that the content of your writing is fine, but the quantity needs to increase. In this case, you can take further practice tests and simply work to write faster.

Start Work Early

Many people find studying in the morning works best for them. Try this yourself and see if you can join the club. Getting your studies out of the way first thing is an excellent way to get more studying done.

Starting work early is often easier because there is less chance of getting distracted and becoming involved doing other things. Watching TV, Internet browsing, or relaxing with friends are often best left until after you have done your studying. These activities then become rewards instead of distractions, and you can enjoy the rest of the day without worry that you should have done more. Studying earlier in the day within a definite "time box," before you have a chance to get distracted by anything else, is a great way to increase the efficiency of your studying and enjoy your days more.

Have Fun Away From Your Studies

If you work intelligently, there is no need to work non-stop. Plan many breaks, and arrange for fun! Enjoyable activities boost your focus and memory. In the same way that muscles need rest after exercise to grow, so too your mind needs to relax after it is exerted.

It is helpful to get as far away as possible from your study and work habits. Take time to travel to another city, another country, or simply try to do something new. Getting away and having fun will mean that when you do return to studying, you will be completely ready to learn, to work hard, and get the best grades you are capable of.

Create Study Routines: 60-60-30, 50-50-10

Creating definite study routines will allow you to better manage your time. It is difficult and unsustainable to work constantly for hours at a time, so implement regular patterns in which you alternate between working and taking breaks. This is short-scale time boxing applied to a rigorous work/rest pattern.

Experiment with what works best for you as different stretches of concentration work well for different people. Some prefer a longer four hour work session to get into "flow," while others prefer shorter ones so as to never feel overwhelmed by a project.

An example work/rest study routine that fits well into a normal day is to work for a 50 minute period followed by a 10 minute break, and every four hours take an hour break for a meal.

However, there are no hard and fast rules. You might prefer to work for 90 minutes at a time, and then take a 30 minute break. The aim is to find what works well for you so that you can sustain working for a long period of time with good focus and minimum fatigue.

If you feel exhausted or too mentally strained with a routine, then work for smaller cycles. You can always increase the work time lengths if it seems doable later.

Make sure to always use a timer, and stop working when it sounds, even if you want to continue. You often won't be aware that you need a break when you actually do. If you become successful with this habit, you will find you can create work-rest routines that are generative and allow you to work with focus for 6, 8, 10, or even 12 hour days whilst still feeling good.

Minimize Possible Distractions and Eliminate Multi-Tasking

One of the greatest enemies to successful work in the modern age is the abundance of distractions. When you are studying, it is imperative to make sure that you study and do nothing else. Your ability to focus all of your attention on the task at hand is a powerful asset. Attempting to do more than one thing at a time or switching between activities jeopardizes this.

Turn off your mobile phone and close the internet browser. If these remain a possible distraction, make it as difficult as possible to access them. For example, turn off your phone and put it out of sight or out of reach. Consider giving it to a friend or leaving it in another room until you are finished working.

These distractions will compromise how effectively you work, and even worse, can lead to you stopping work altogether. Just checking a website or your phone for a moment can cause a series of internal triggers, and in no time you will lose the motivation and focus you had. This can be a big obstacle for students and employees alike. If this sounds like your past studying attempts, make eliminating distractions a priority.

Set Goals for Grades

Setting goals for the grades you want will make it easier to ascertain the level of work required to receive them. The goal of simply "getting the best grades you can" is good, but not good enough. These goals need to be more specific and ideally very specific. Many students already have goals for the grades they want to achieve. If you don't have any, start thinking about what yours could be now.

Having clear goals for the grades you want will make it easier to ascertain what you need to learn in order to achieve them. This is partly achieved by saving you from wasting time learning things you don't need to. Some skills and information might take a lot of time to learn, but if they are beyond what you need to learn it will be a waste of time. For example, for an essay-based exam, there is no use learning a large amount of quotations (enough to get an A) if your target is a B grade and your grasp of concepts isn't nearly strong enough to get a B.

Goals for grades will also allow you to celebrate successes and push you to do more when needed.

Once you have decided what your target grades are, find out precisely what you need to work on in order to achieve them. Then build your study schedule around working on these areas (with regular testing to ensure you are progressing well).

Clarify Study Session Goals

Every time you sit down to study, you should be clear about what you are going to do and what you want to gain from the session. Planning to "study for module A" won't be nearly as effective as "50 minutes reading and annotating chapter 1." It is far too easy to study aimlessly while naively believing that you are learning. Working in this fuzzy, diffused way will often mean you don't learn or progress in your work. Instead, have focused, clear targets each time you sit.

At the end of the study session, you will also be able to check off the task, and this will also help you feel more motivated to continue on. The sense of incremental progress with each completed study session will build momentum and make each successive study session easier.

Detach from Work While on Breaks

When you take a short break from work, it is very important that you really do take a break.

If you are studying at a computer screen (perhaps you are writing up some lecture notes), the break you take must be away from the computer. If you are taking only 10 minute breaks every hour, it is important to make this break a time for your mind and body to separate from what you have been working on.

If you are working at a computer, opening a new browser and checking a news channel or a social networking site is no longer working, but is it truly taking a break? Not really. Instead, move away from the desk and away from the computer. Do something physical. Maybe take a walk or lie down. At the very least, don't look at a screen. The break needs to be spent on something different from what you have been doing. If you have been sitting at a computer screen, lying down outside on the grass for 10 minutes could help you to unwind sufficiently.

You might find it helpful to engage your mind with something else altogether. If you don't engage your mind with something else, like a video game or book, you might find your mind racing on with what you were doing. To get more mental separation and a better break, consider doing something that takes your attention away from what you were working on altogether.

Why are you at School/College/University?

Knowing exactly what you want from your course and what you are going to do afterward will further help you to focus and study well.

Perhaps you are career-driven and want to go into a certain industry after your course. If this is the case, research the job role you want, how much money you want to be earning, where you want to work, etc. Getting details will help you feel grounded and motivated to continue on with the course.

For some students, there is no definite job role at the end. This does not mean that you cannot find a clear purpose for studying hard. Maybe you enjoy the subject and want to study it for this reason alone. If this is the case, consider concrete things you can do to get more from it. This could be getting an article in your field published.

Understanding why you are studying and what you really want from your course is a great way to further boost your focus and enjoyment.

Find a Study Partner and/or a Study Group

Studying with other people is a great way to get more from your course.

Depending on your preferences for working and your personality, this can be a fantastic prospect or a daunting one. However, creating a study group, or at the very least one person with whom you regularly work, can help a lot. Explaining topics and quizzing one another will boost your comprehension and ensure that you thoroughly understand the material.

Make sure you choose the right people to study with. It might not be best to study with a friend you also go out partying with. Additionally, make sure you study with people of a similar ability. 'Carrying' someone who is struggling won't be productive.

Working in a group can be a brilliant idea as well. This can be the most enjoyable way to work, especially if you are naturally highly social. Working in a group helps you to motivate one another and can provide many points of view.

Perfect Necessary Skills and Seek Feedback

There will inevitably be skills within your subject you need to master. These skills will usually require someone else to critique your ability. Seek as much feedback as possible in order to improve these skills.

Whether you are working in a laboratory or writing essays, the skills you have to develop cannot be marked and improved on entirely by yourself. You need an expert. This person will often be a teacher assigned to you. It might then be a matter of luck how helpful their critiques are and whether they are offered as regularly as you require them. If they aren't offered enough or aren't helpful enough, seek another tutor from the establishment to replace and/or work alongside to provide extra help.

In cases such as essay writing, you will need to practice regularly. Practice even if your work won't be marked. The more feedback you can get the better, so it doesn't hurt to ask other teachers to critique your work as well.

Whatever the skill set you are trying to develop, practice properly, practice regularly, seek feedback and then improve. Use this process again and again, until you develop your skill set into an art form.

Build a Relationship with a Tutor/Mentor

Having a go-between for you and your school/establishment will prove very helpful. Many centers will provide you with a 'tutor,' i.e., someone you meet with regularly in order to discuss your progress. If yours doesn't provide this extra help, find someone who can take on this role for you.

Your tutor can provide guidance for your course and let you know what to expect. He or she can answer questions on any number of things. For example, a tutor might help you to find old exam papers to work from, or find out where an exam will be seated.

If anything goes wrong during your course and you need help (perhaps you fall ill and need an extension on a project), help and advice from your tutor could be essential. Also, if you have moved away from home and need guidance on everyday issues, for example, money management, eating out, etc. Having someone older who can guide you will make life easier.

Thank you

Thank you for making it to the end of both books. If you enjoyed them, please leave a review on the Amazon website.

All the best,

John Connelly

55170344R00054

Made in the USA
Middletown, DE
16 July 2019